God is Good

PSALM 34

BIBLE CHAPTERS
FOR KIDS

I will always say
good things about
God, and talk about
how great he is.

"I will bless the Lord at
all times; his praise will
continually be in my mouth."

(verse 1)

When I'm
feeling down, I
know God's power
can help me feel
stronger.

"My soul will make her boast in
the Lord: the humble will hear
it and be glad."

(verse 2)

Let's worship
God together, and
talk about how
wonderful he is.

"O magnify the Lord with
me, and let us exalt his
name together."

(verse 3)

When I pray to
God, he hears me
and I no longer
feel afraid.

"I sought the Lord, and he
heard me, and delivered me
from all my fears."

(verse 4)

When God
is in my life,
I feel proud
of myself.

"They looked to him, and
were lightened: and their
faces were not ashamed."

(verse 5)

When I have
problems, I can
pray, and God
will help me.

"This poor man cried, and the Lord heard him, and saved him out of all his troubles."

(verse 6)

God's angels
are all around
me, and they
protect me.

"The angel of the Lord encamps
round about them that fear him,
and delivers them."

(verse 7)

All my senses
tell me that
God is good
and will watch
over me.

"O taste and see that the Lord
is good: blessed is the man
that trusts in him."

(verse 8)

I respect
God, so he takes
excellent care
of me.

Even strong animals sometimes go hungry, but those who pray to God will always have what they need.

"The young lions lack and suffer hunger: but they that seek the Lord will not want any good thing."

(verse 10)

I love to
read the Bible.
It teaches
me how I can
worship God.

"Come, you children,
hearken to me: I will teach
you the fear of the Lord."

(verse 11)

I want my
days to be happy,
so I try not to
speak bad
about others.

"What man is he that desires life,
and loves many days, that he may see
good? Keep your tongue from evil,"

(verse 12)

And always
tell the truth.

"And your lips from
speaking deceit."

(verse 13)

I want to do
the right thing,
so I try my best
to be kind
to others.

"Turn away from evil, and do good;
seek peace, and pursue it."

(verse 14)

God keeps his eye on me. God is there when I need him.

"The eyes of the Lord are on the righteous, and his ears are open to their cry."

(verse 15)

More books in the series:

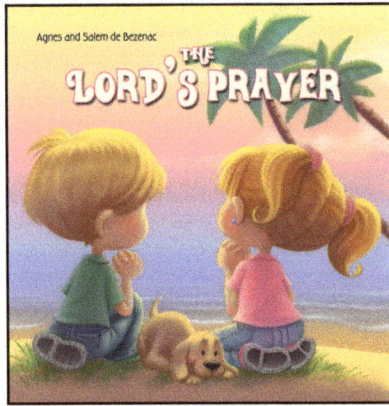

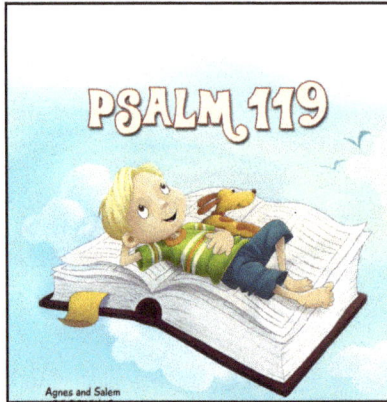

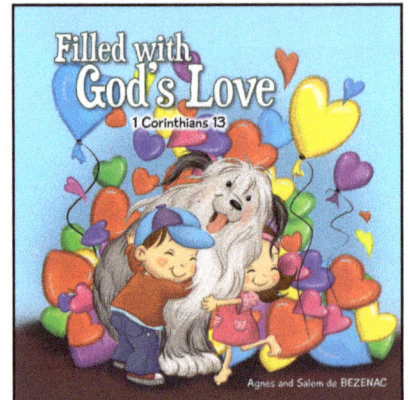

The Lord's Prayer

PSALM 119

SAFE WITH GOD — Psalm 91

PROVERBS

My Shepherd — Psalm 23

Filled with God's Love — 1 Corinthians 13

iCHARACTER

Published by iCharacter Ltd. (Ireland)
www.icharacter.org
By Agnes and Salem de Bezenac
Illustrated by Agnes de Bezenac
Colored by SPORG Studio
Copyright. All rights reserved.
All Bible verses adapted from the KJV.

www.ingramcontent.com/pod-product-compliance
Lightning Source LLC
Chambersburg PA
CBHW040250100426
42811CB00011B/1219